The Easy Keyboard Library 

Nat King Cole

20 classic songs for keyboard

Published 2004

Music arranged & engraved by Artemis Music Limited (www.artemismusic.com)
Cover Image Michael Ochs Archives / Redferns Music Picture Library

Griffin House 161 Hammersmith Road London England W6 8BS

(I Love You) For Sentimental Reasons

Words by Derek Watson
Music by William Best

Suggested Registration: Piano
Rhythm: Swing Ballad
Tempo: ♩ = 80

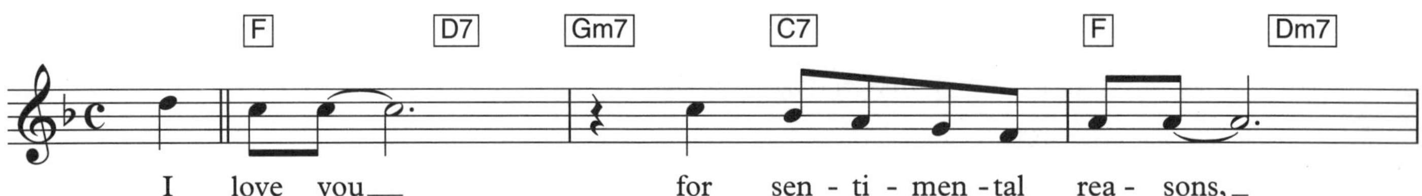

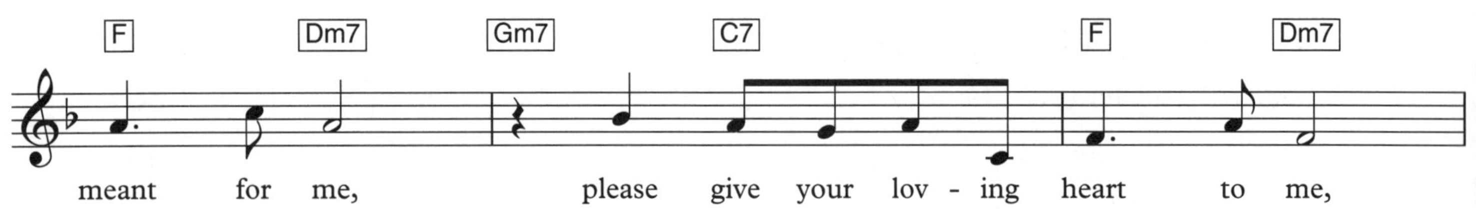

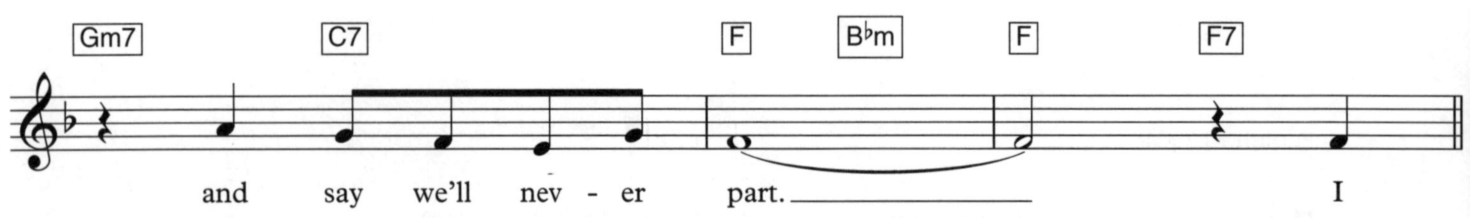

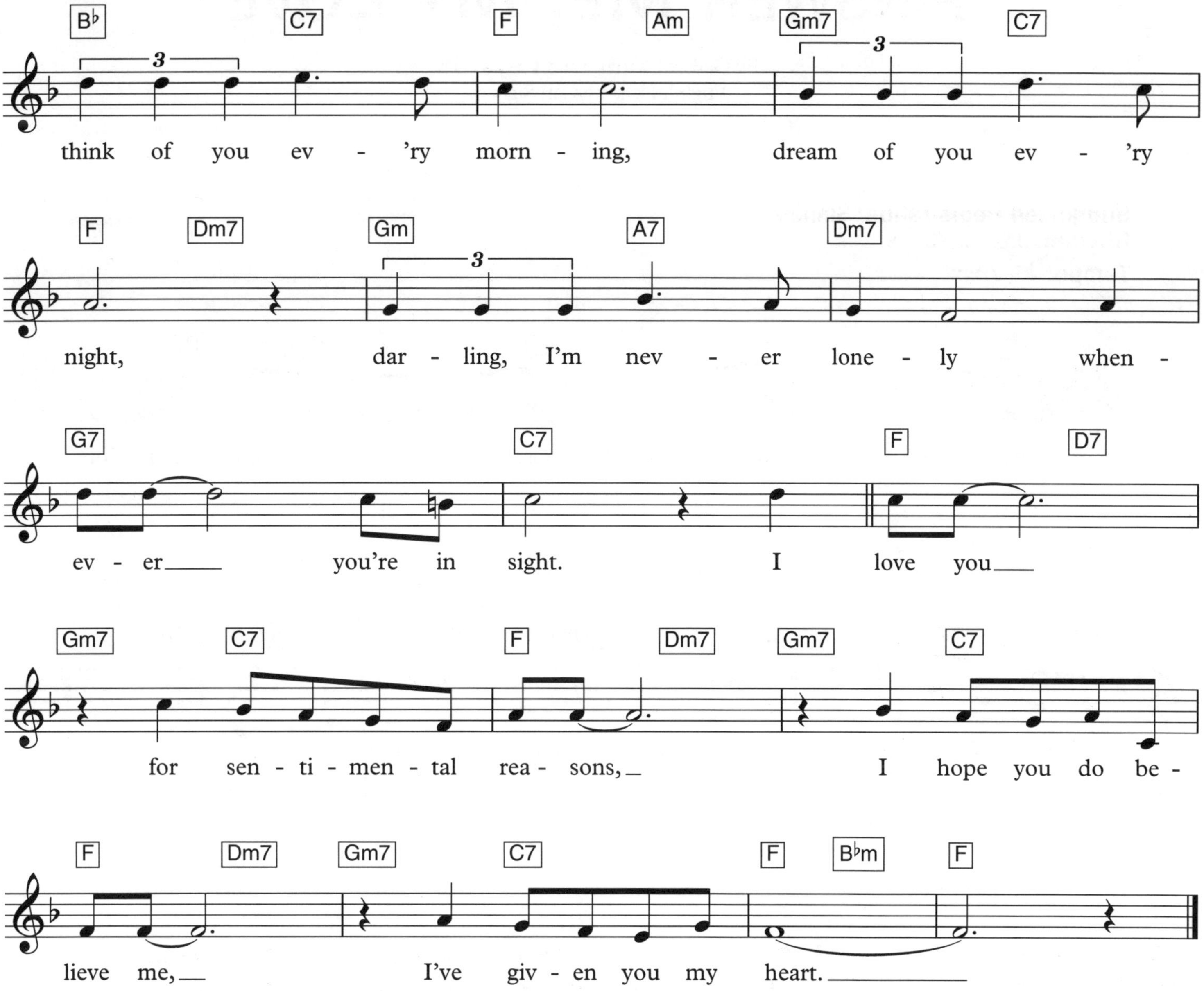

B♭ C7 F Am Gm7 C7
3 3
think of you ev - 'ry morn - ing, dream of you ev - 'ry
F Dm7 Gm A7 Dm7
3
night, dar - ling, I'm nev - er lone - ly when -
G7 C7 F D7
ev - er you're in sight. I love you
Gm7 C7 F Dm7 Gm7 C7
for sen - ti - men - tal rea - sons, I hope you do be -
F Dm7 Gm7 C7 F B♭m F
lieve me, I've giv - en you my heart.

F
D7
Gm7
C7
Dm7
B♭m
F7
B♭
Am
Gm
A7
G7

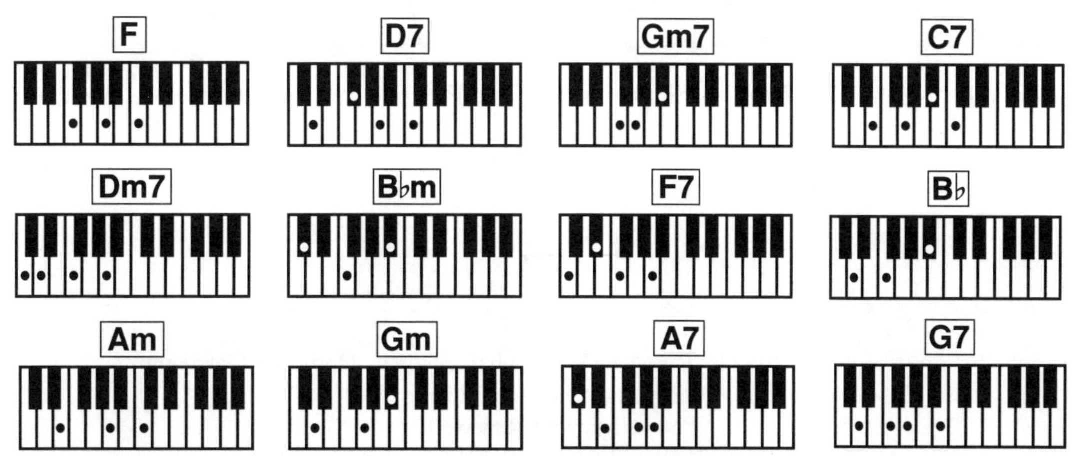

Answer Me, My Love

By Gerhard Winkler and Fred Rauch
English Lyric by Carl Sigman

Suggested Registration: Strings
Rhythm: Jazz waltz
Tempo: ♩ = 70

G D Ddim Em7 A7 D
Tell me how I came to lose your love? Please an - swer me, my love.

F♯m
D7
F♯m
If you're hap - pi - er with - out me, I'll try not to care.

Dm
E7
A7
But if you still think a - bout me, please lis - ten to my prayer.

D
A
G
Gm
D
You must know I've been true, won't you say that we can start a - new?

G
D
Ddim
Em7
A7
D
In my sor - row now I turn to you, please an - swer me, my love.

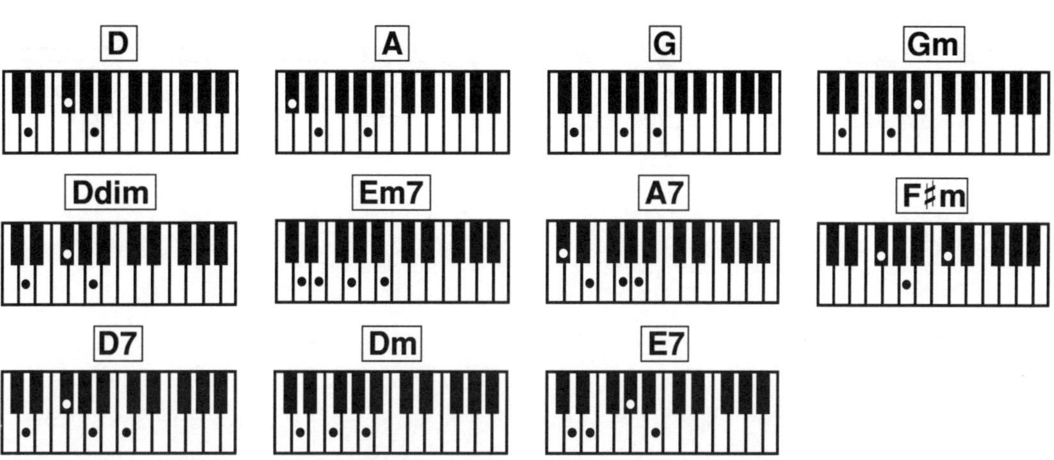
D
A
G
Gm
Ddim
Em7
A7
F♯m
D7
Dm
E7

Around The World

Words by Harold Adamson
Music by Victor Young

Suggested Registration: Violin
Rhythm: Ballad Waltz
Tempo: ♩ = 100

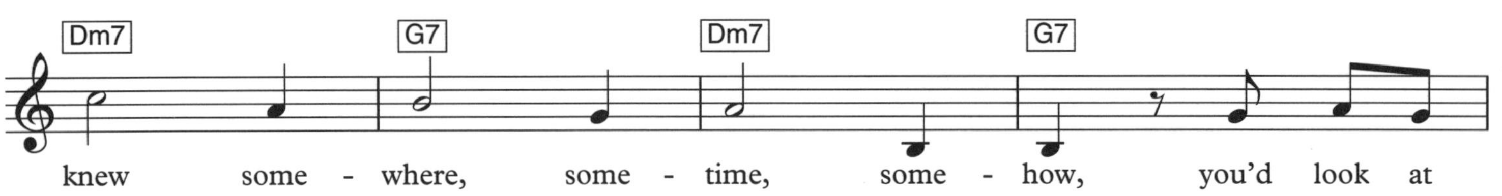

C
might have been in Coun - ty Down, or in New

A7
Dm7
York, or gay Pa - ris, or ev - en Lon - don town. No

F
F♯dim
C
A7
more will I go all a - round the world, for I have

Dm7
G7
C
found my world in you.

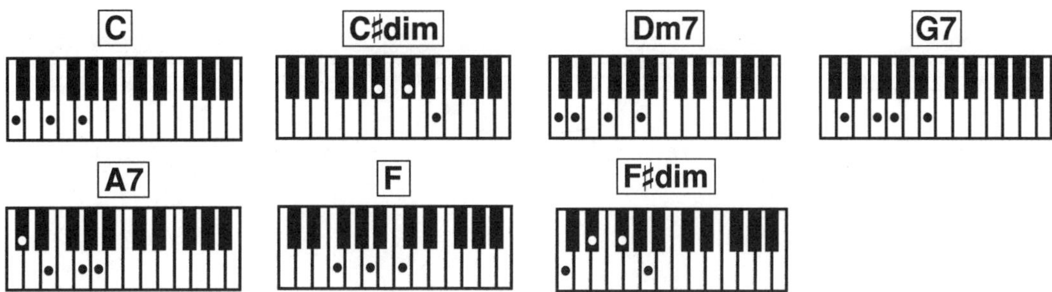
C
C♯dim
Dm7
G7
A7
F
F♯dim

Because You're Mine

Words by Sammy Cahn
Music by Nicholas Brodsky

Suggested Registration: Strings
Rhythm: Jazz waltz
Tempo: ♩ = 65

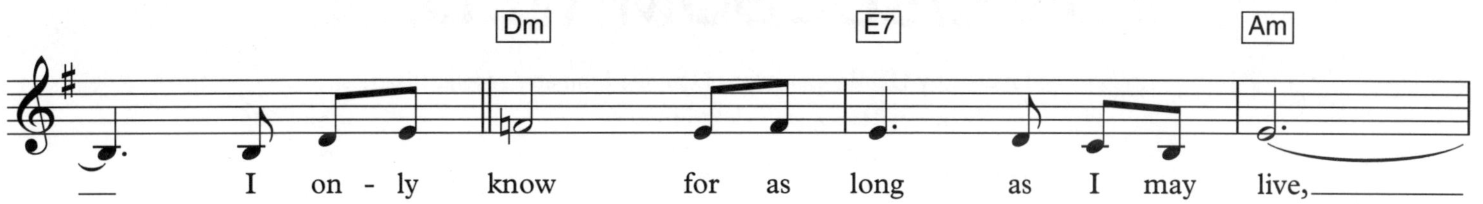
Dm
E7
Am
I on - ly know for as long as I may live,

Em
F♯7
Bm
I'll on - ly live for the kiss that you a - lone may

Am7
D7
G
give me. And when we kiss that is - n't thun-der dear, it's on - ly my poor

Dm
E7
Am7
D7
G
heart you hear, and it's ap - plause, be - cause you're mine.

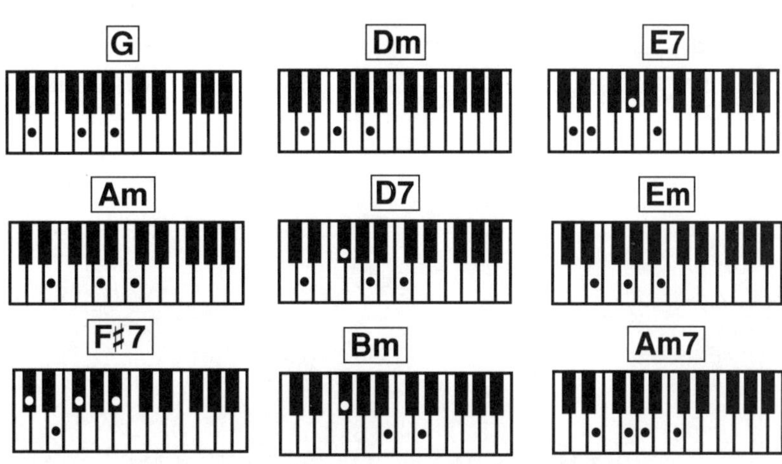
G
Dm
E7
Am
D7
Em
F♯7
Bm
Am7

A BLOSSOM FELL

Words and Music by Harold Cornelius, Dominic John and Howard Barnes

Suggested Registration: Oboe
Rhythm: Ballad
Tempo: ♩ = 85

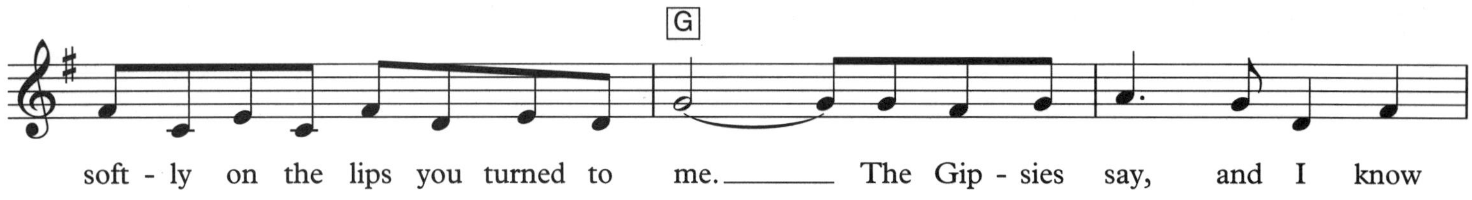

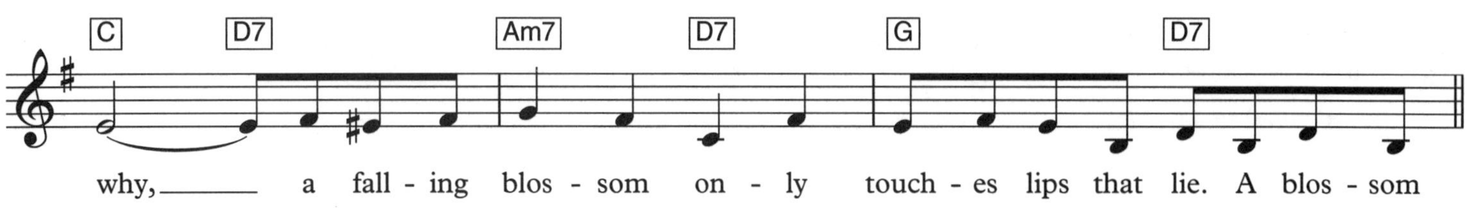

G
C
G
moon. I thought you loved me, you said you loved me, we planned to -

D7
G
C
B7
ge - ther, to dream for - ev - er. The dream has end - ed, for true love

Em7
A7
D7
G
died, the night a blos - som fell and touched two lips that lied.

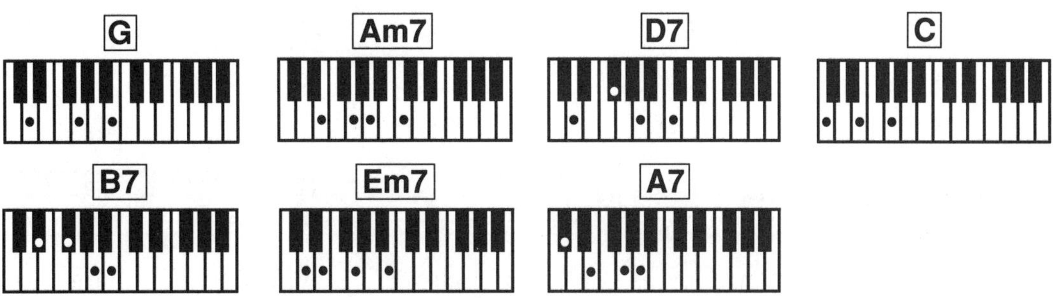
G
Am7
D7
C
B7
Em7
A7

The Christmas Song (Chestnuts Roasting On An Open Fire)

Words and Music by Mel Tormé and Robert Wells

Suggested Registration: French Horn
Rhythm: Ballad
Tempo: ♩ = 65

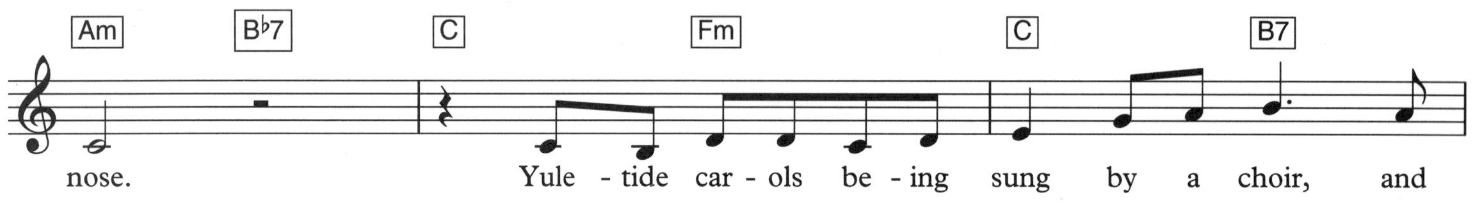

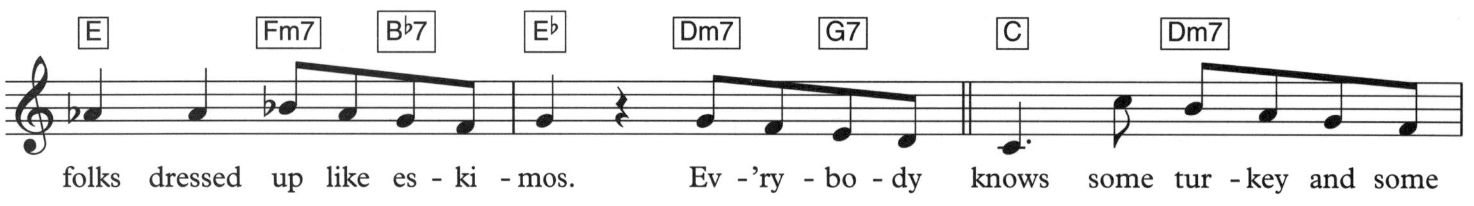

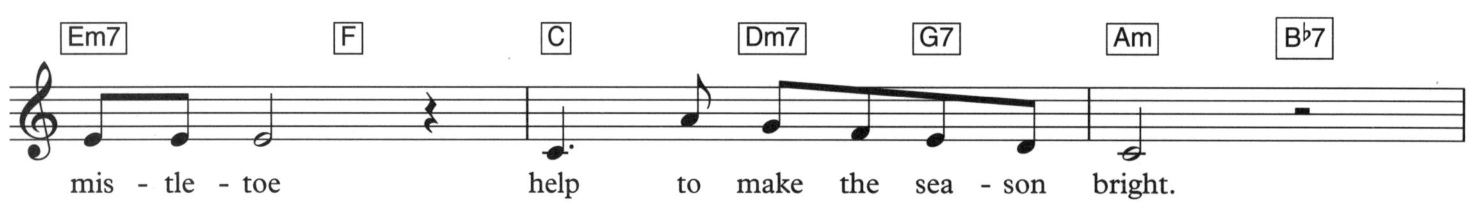

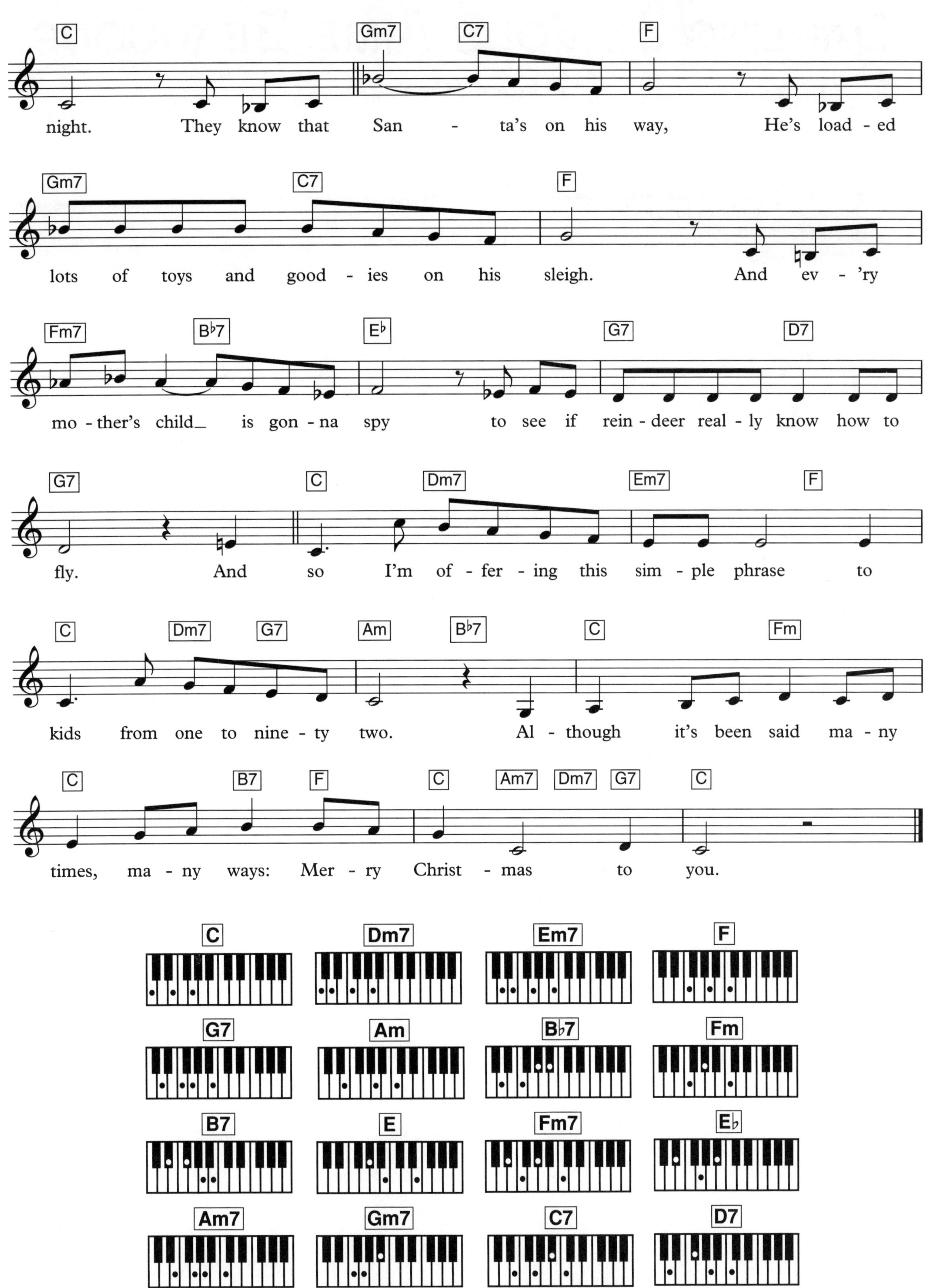
C Gm7 C7 F
night. They know that San - ta's on his way, He's load - ed
Gm7 C7 F
lots of toys and good - ies on his sleigh. And ev - 'ry
Fm7 B♭7 E♭ G7 D7
mo - ther's child_ is gon - na spy to see if rein - deer real - ly know how to
G7 C Dm7 Em7 F
fly. And so I'm of - fer - ing this sim - ple phrase to
C Dm7 G7 Am B♭7 C Fm
kids from one to nine - ty two. Al - though it's been said ma - ny
C B7 F C Am7 Dm7 G7 C
times, ma - ny ways: Mer - ry Christ - mas to you.
C
Dm7
Em7
F
G7
Am
B♭7
Fm
B7
E
Fm7
E♭
Am7
Gm7
C7
D7

Darling Je Vous Aime Beaucoup

Words and Music by Anna Sosenko

Suggested Registration: Flute
Rhythm: Ballad
Tempo: ♩ = 80

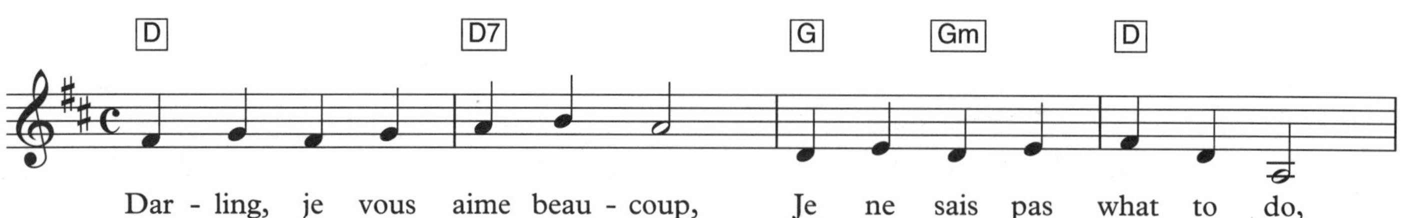

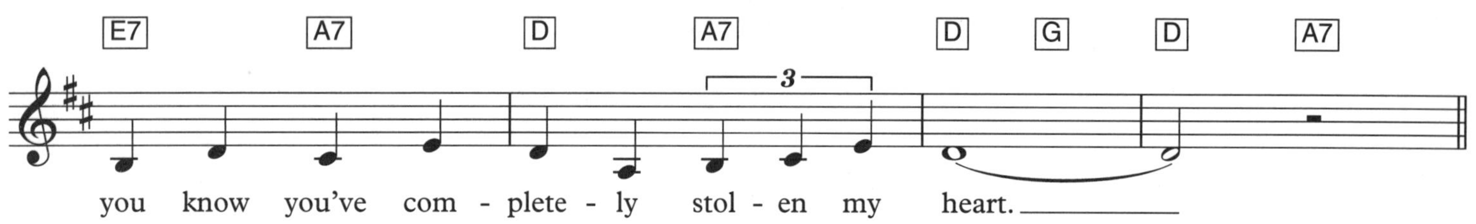

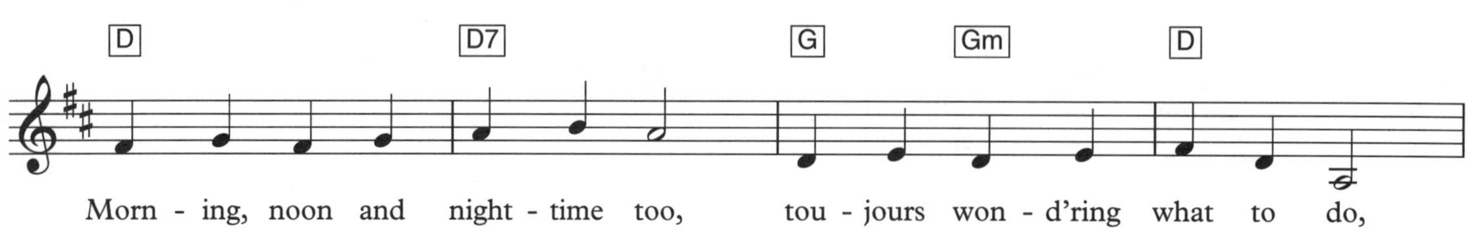

G
Gm
D
Ah, Cher - ie! My love for you is très, très fort;
Bm
F♯7
Bm
E7
A7
wish my French were good e- nough, I'd tell you so much more.

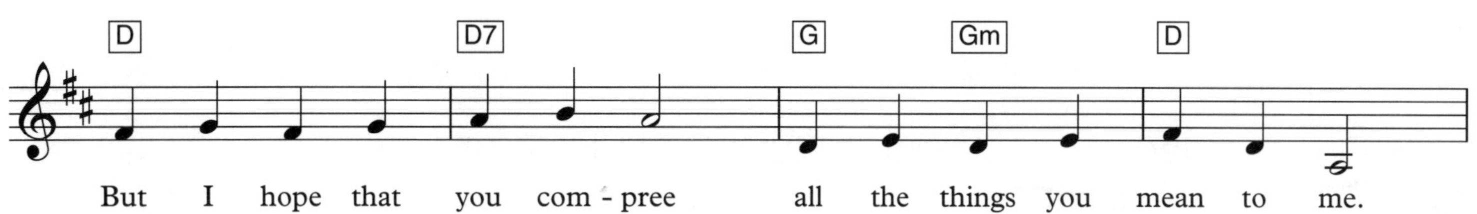
D
D7
G
Gm
D
But I hope that you com - pree all the things you mean to me.

E7
A7
D
A7
D
A7
D
Dar - ling, je vous aime beau - coup, I love you, yes I do.

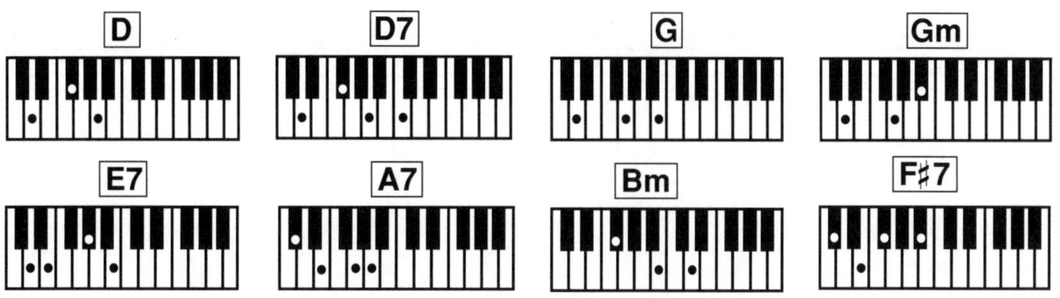
D
D7
G
Gm
E7
A7
Bm
F♯7

If I May

Words and Music by Charles Singleton and Rose Marie McCoy

Suggested Registration: Saxophone
Rhythm: Swing
Tempo: ♩ = 105

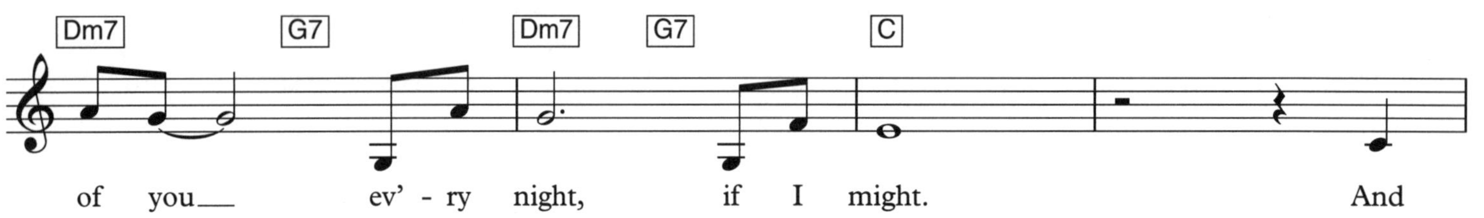

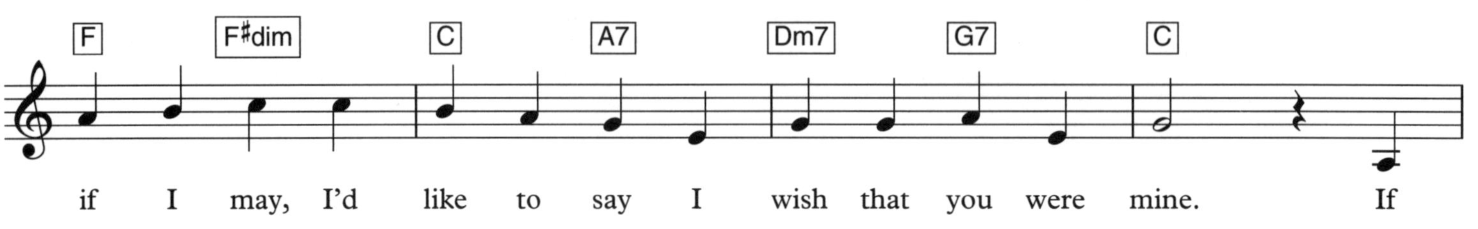

Dm7
G7
Dm7
G7
C
tell you___ of your charms ev - 'ry day, if I may. I'd like to

Dm7
G7
Dm7
G7
C
hold you___ in my arms ev - 'ry night if I might. You're the

F
F♯dim
C
B♭7
A7
3
ob - ject of my af - fec - tions, and if you have no ob - jec - tions, I'd like to

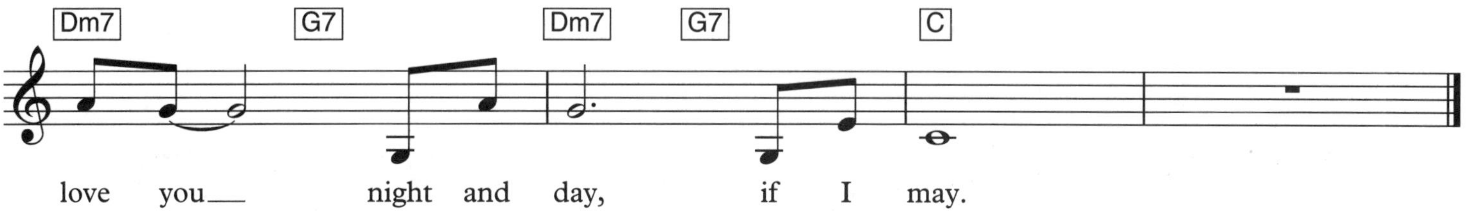
Dm7
G7
Dm7
G7
C
love you___ night and day, if I may.

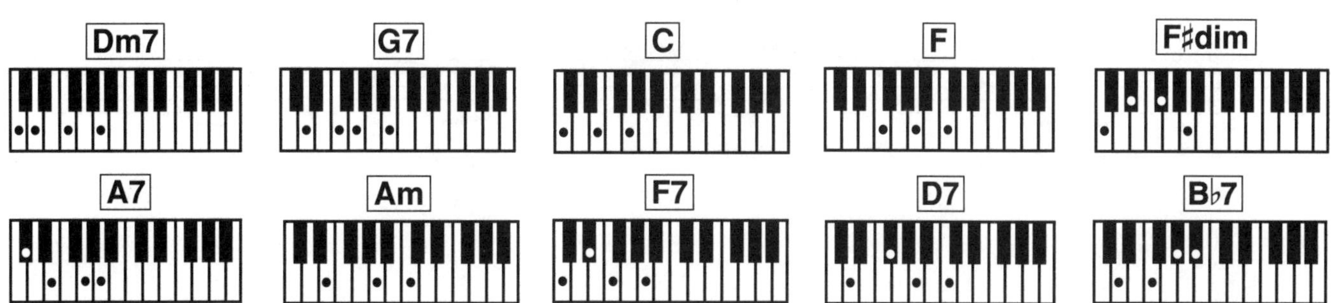
Dm7
G7
C
F
F♯dim
A7
Am
F7
D7
B♭7

It's Only A Paper Moon

Words by E Y Harburg and Billy Rose
Music by Harold Arlen

Suggested Registration: Piano
Rhythm: Medium swing
Tempo: ♩ = 130

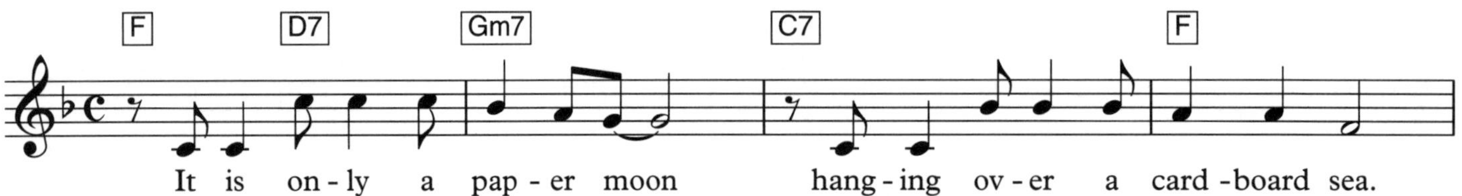

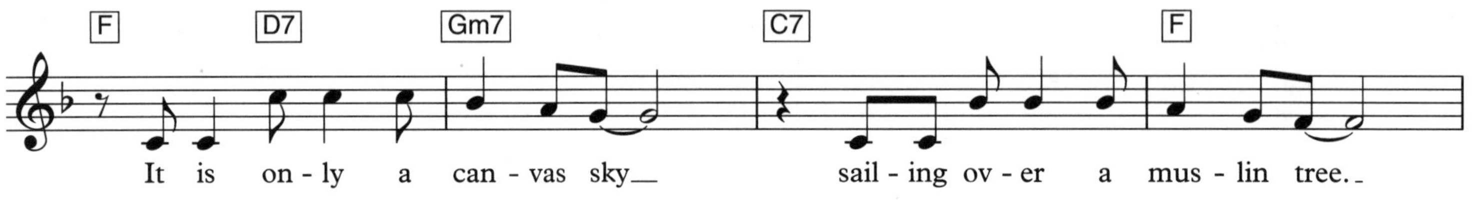

B♭ Bdim F Gm7 C7 F F7
out your love, it's a hon - ky - tonk pa - rade. With -

B♭ Bdim F D7 Gm7 C7
out your love, it's a me - lo - dy played on a pen - ny ar- cade.

F D7 Gm7 C7 F
It's a Bar - num and Bail - ey world, just as pho - ney as it can be.

F D7 Gm7 C7 F
But it would - n't be make be - lieve if you be - lieve in me.

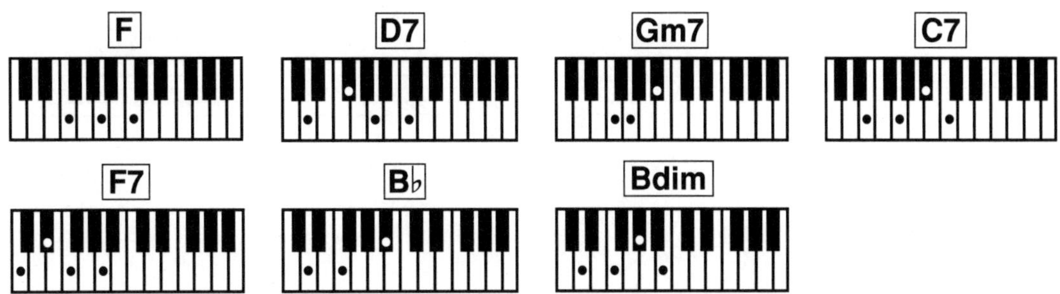
F D7 Gm7 C7
F7 B♭ Bdim

Let There Be Love

Words by Ian Grant
Music by Lionel Rand

Suggested Registration: Trumpet
Rhythm: Swing
Tempo: ♩ = 120

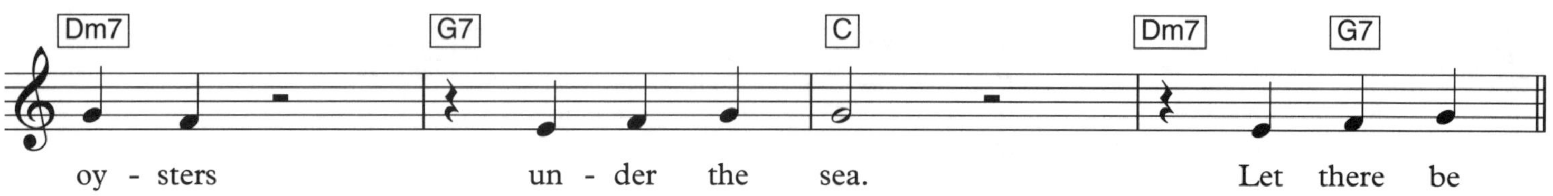

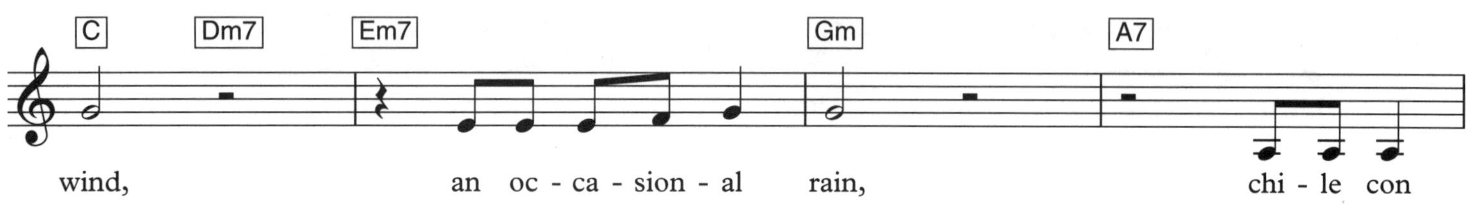

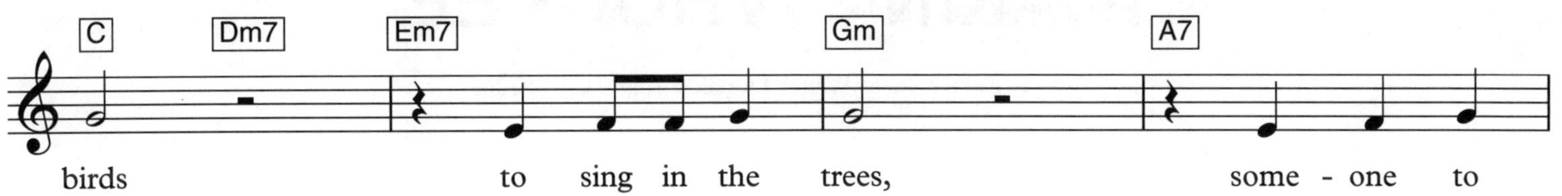
C
Dm7
Em7
Gm
A7
birds to sing in the trees, some - one to

Dm7
G7
C
G7
bless me when - ev - er I sneeze. Let there be

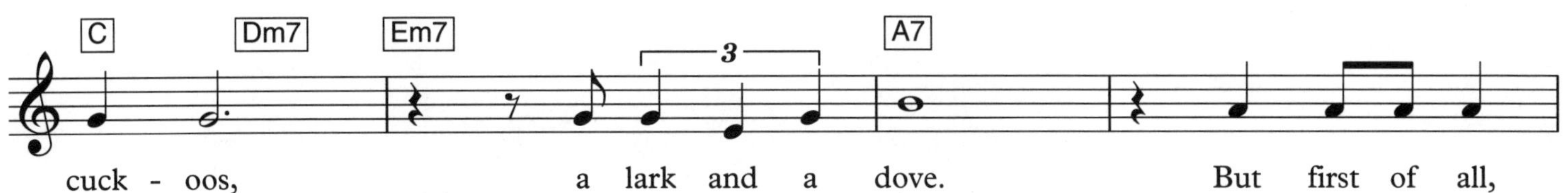
C
Dm7
Em7
3
A7
cuck - oos, a lark and a dove. But first of all,

Dm7
G7
C
F
C
please let there be love.

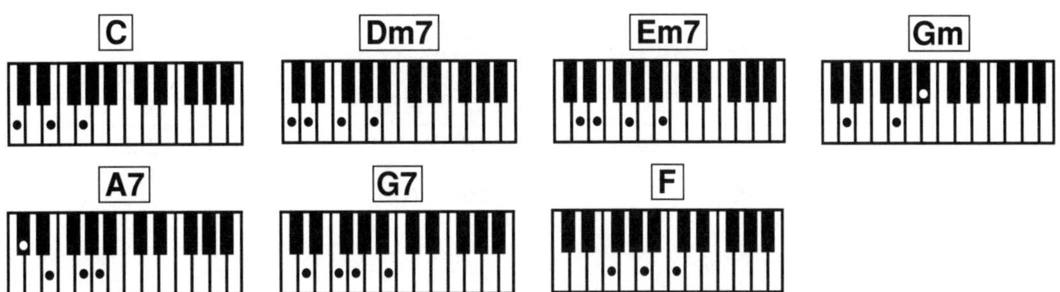
C
Dm7
Em7
Gm
A7
G7
F

Makin' Whoopee

Words and Music by Walter Donaldson and Gus Kahn

Suggested Registration: Trombone
Rhythm: Medium Swing
Tempo: ♩ = 75

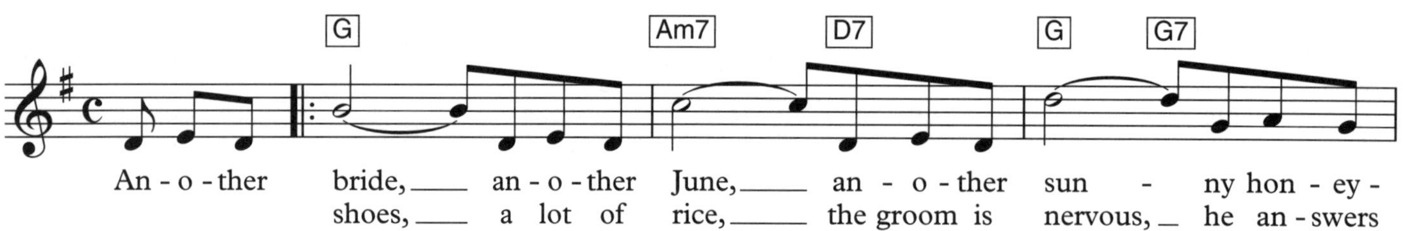

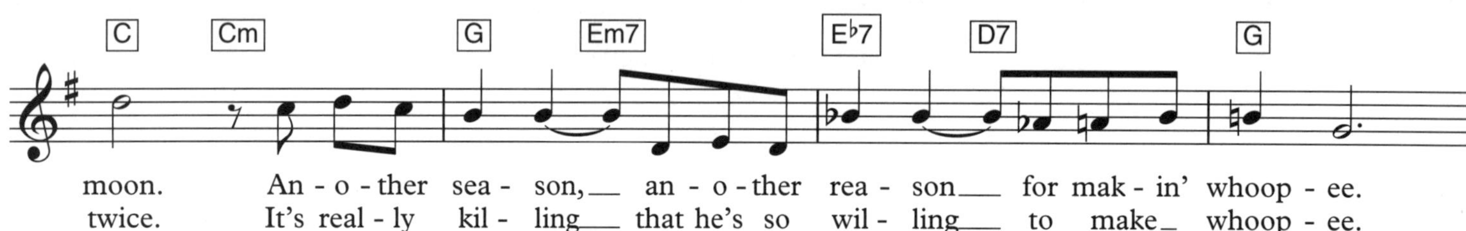

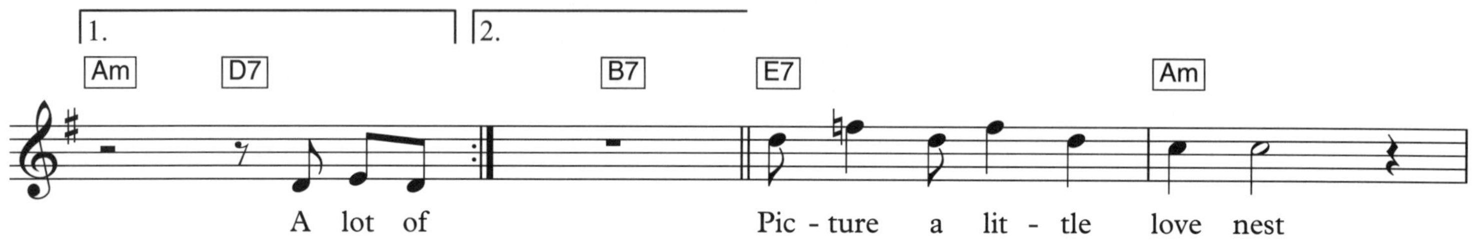

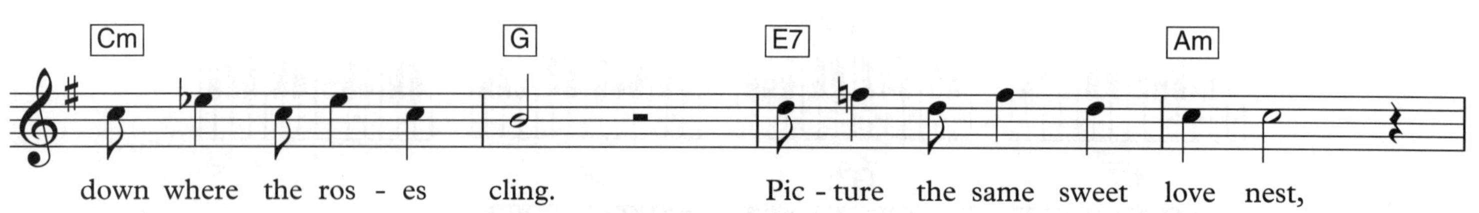

Cm
G
D7
G
see what a year can bring. He's wash - ing dish - es___ and ba - by

Am7
D7
G
G7
C
Cm
clothes,___ he's so am - bi - tious,___ he ev - en sews. But don't for -

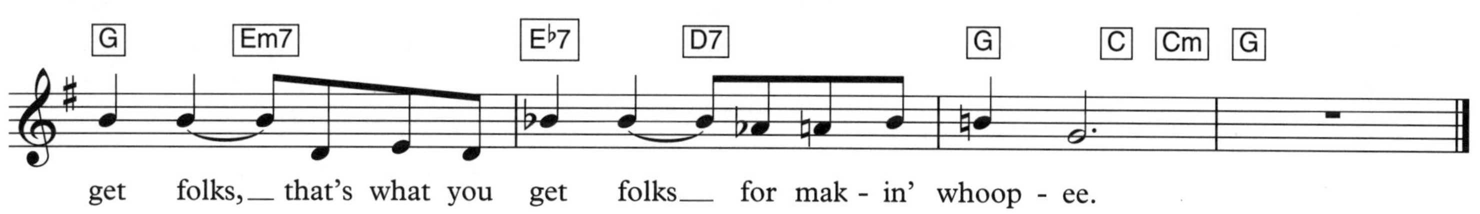
G
Em7
E♭7
D7
G
C
Cm
G
get folks,___ that's what you get folks___ for mak - in' whoop - ee.

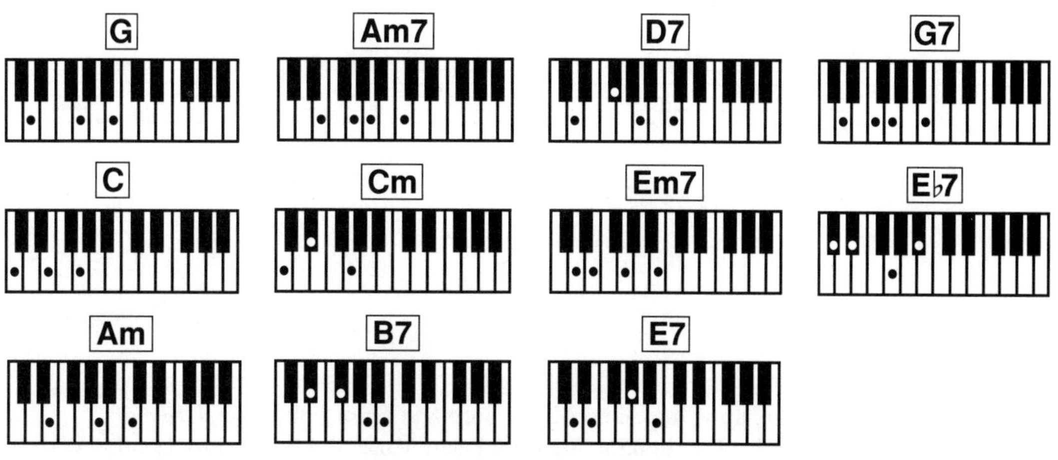
G
Am7
D7
G7
C
Cm
Em7
E♭7
Am
B7
E7

Mother Nature And Father Time

Words and Music by Ben Weisman, Fred Wise and Kay Twomey

Suggested Registration: Clarinet
Rhythm: Ballad
Tempo: ♩ = 75

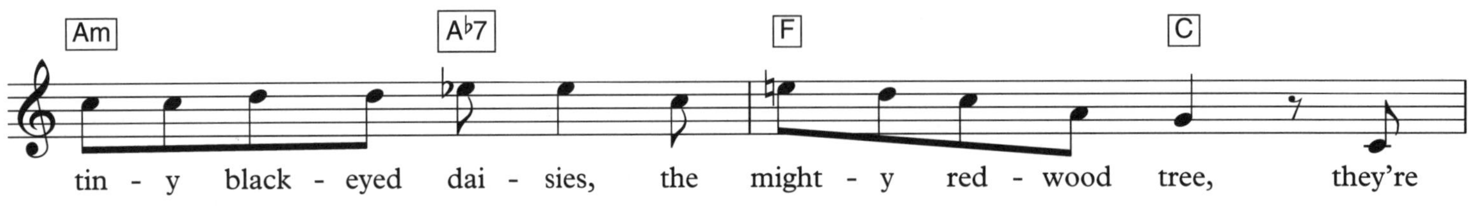

C Caug Am A♭7 F

Dm7 G7 Em7 Am7 D7

NATURE BOY

Words and Music by Eden Ahbez

Suggested Registration: Guitar
Rhythm: Latin
Tempo: ♩ = 100

Dm
A7
Dm
A7
then one day, a mag - ic day he passed my way. And while we spoke of

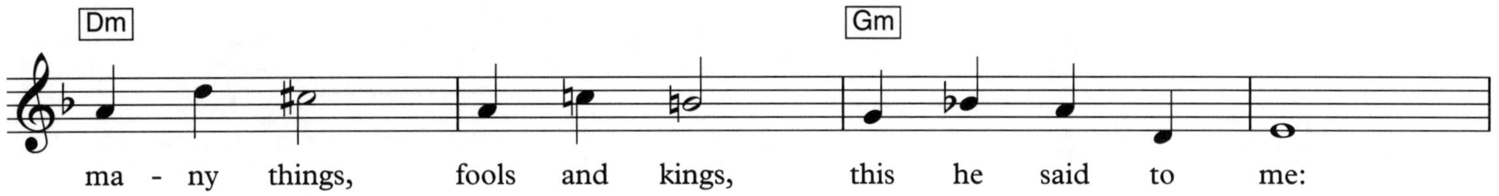
Dm
Gm
ma - ny things, fools and kings, this he said to me:

A7
Dm
"The great - est thing you'll ev - er learn is

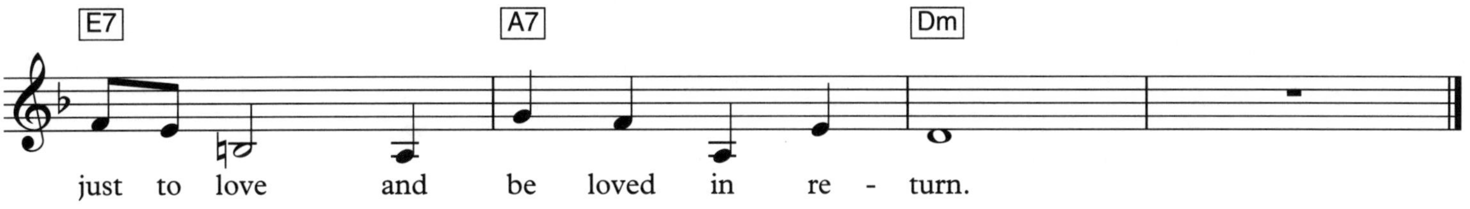
E7
A7
Dm
just to love and be loved in re - turn.

Dm
A7
Gm
E7

Orange Coloured Sky

Words and Music by Milton DeLugg and William Stein

Suggested Registration: Trumpet
Rhythm: Swing
Tempo: ♩ = 110

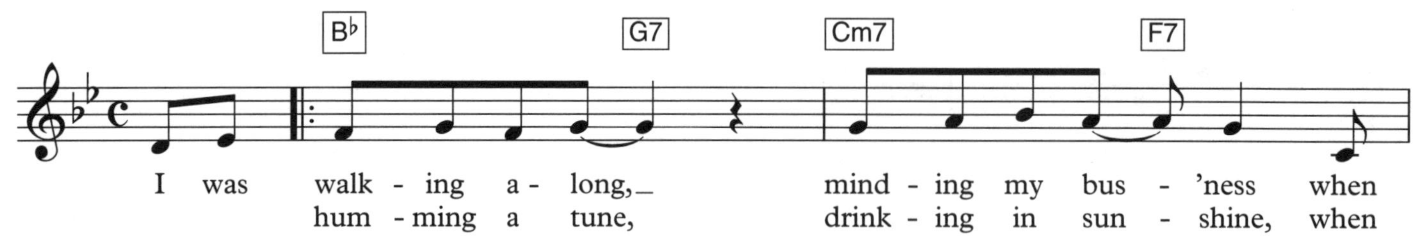

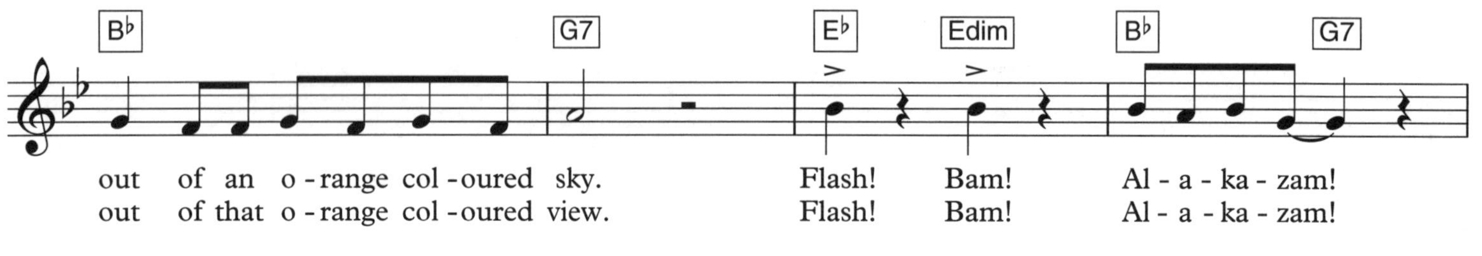

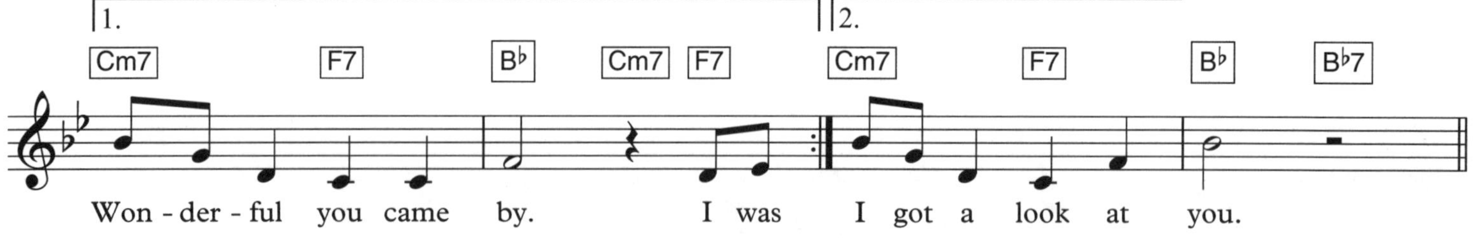

C7
Gm7
F7
3
in - to a spin and I start - ed to shout: "I've been hit, this is it, this is

B♭
G7
Cm7
F7
3
it, I. T. it!" I was walk - ing a - long,_ mind - ing my bus - 'ness when

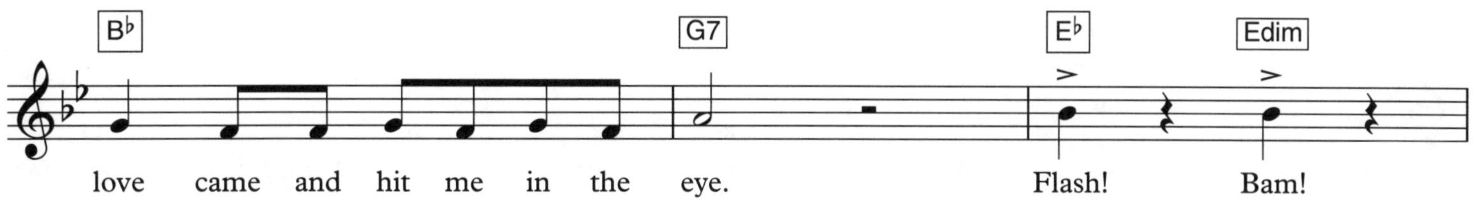
B♭
G7
E♭
Edim
love came and hit me in the eye. Flash! Bam!

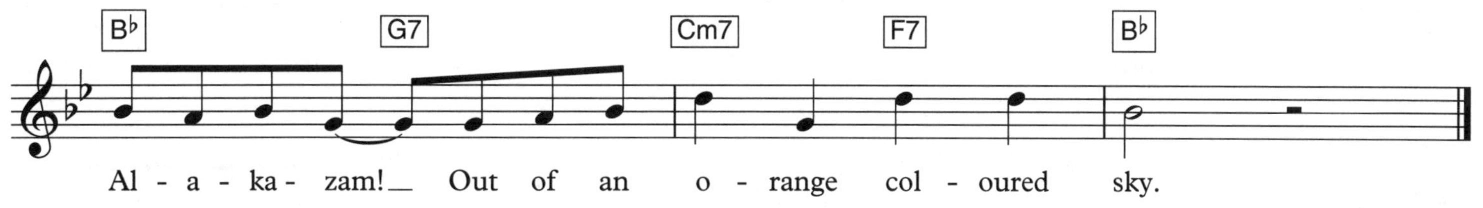
B♭
G7
Cm7
F7
B♭
Al - a - ka - zam!_ Out of an o - range col - oured sky.

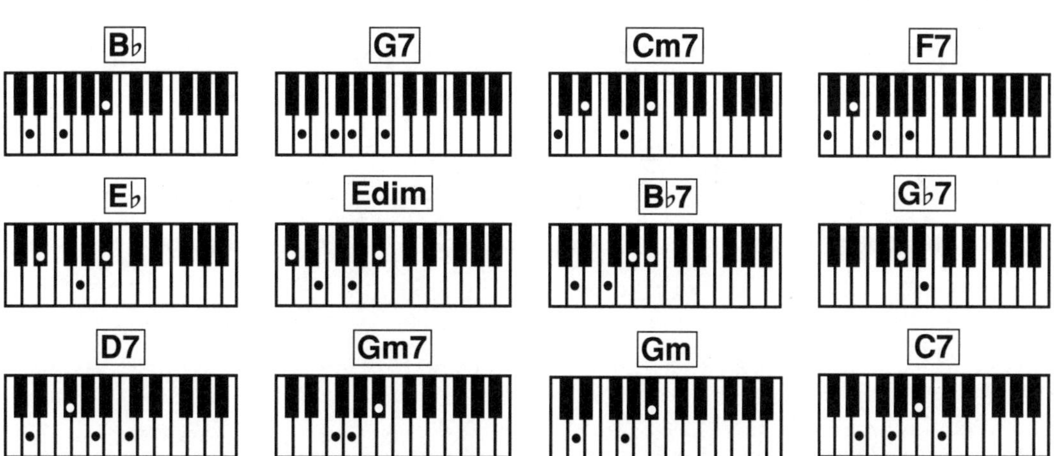
B♭
G7
Cm7
F7
E♭
Edim
B♭7
G♭7
D7
Gm7
Gm
C7

Send For Me

Words and Music by Ollie Jones

Suggested Registration: Saxophone
Rhythm: Rock and Roll
Tempo: ♩ = 115

F
B♭7
F
morn - ing, noon and night, a - in the ear - ly bright, a - don't you fret my pret - ty pet, I'm
F7
B♭7
gon - na treat you right. Don't you dare raise a hair, I'm gon - na
F
C7
B♭7
share your ev - 'ry care. An - y - where, oh yeah, send for
F
F
B♭7
me, I'll be there. An - y - thing that up - sets you, send for
F
B♭7
me, send for me. I'll be there to pro - tect you, wait and
F
C7
see, wait and see. Don't de - lay, right a -
B♭7
F
way, send for me, send for me.
F
B♭7
C7
F7

SMILE

Music by Charles Chaplin
Words by John Turner and Geoffrey Parsons

Suggested Registration: Strings

Rhythm: Ballad

Tempo: ♩ = 85

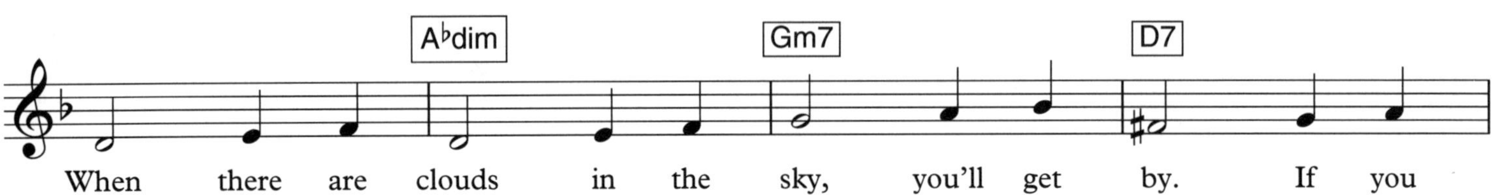

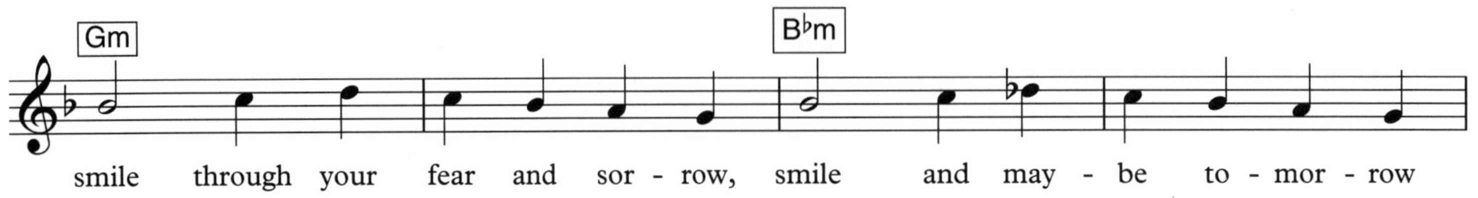

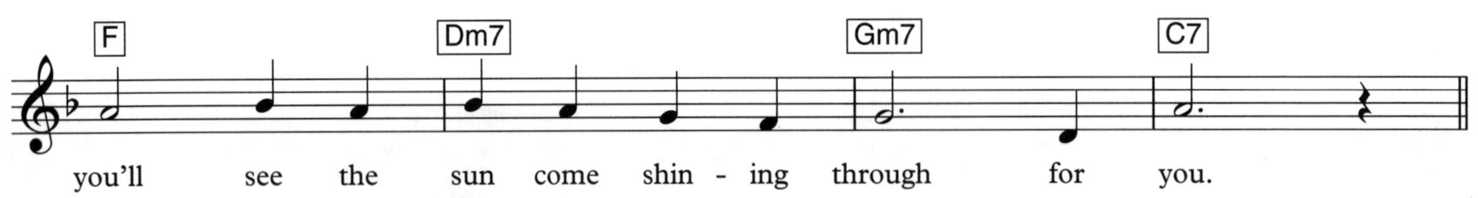

F
Light up your face with glad - ness, hide ev - 'ry trace of sad - ness,

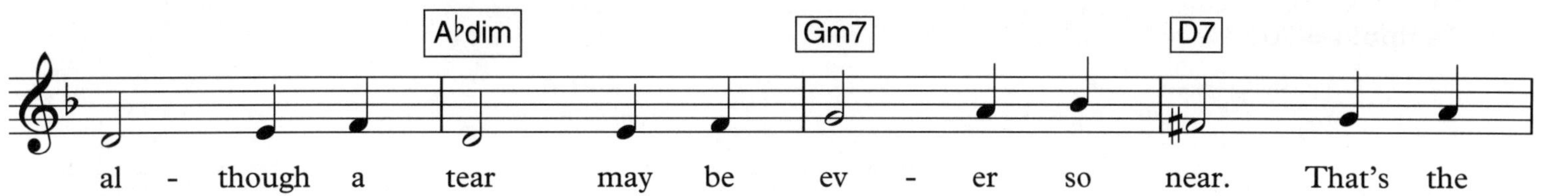
A♭dim
Gm7
D7
al - though a tear may be ev - er so near. That's the

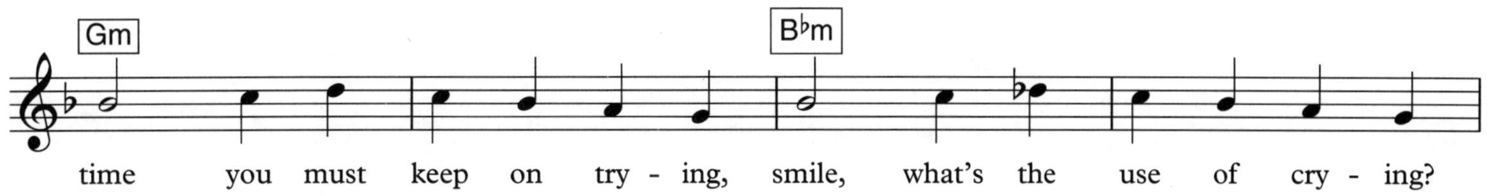
Gm
B♭m
time you must keep on try - ing, smile, what's the use of cry - ing?

F
Dm7
Gm7
C7
F
You'll find that life is still worth - while if you just smile.

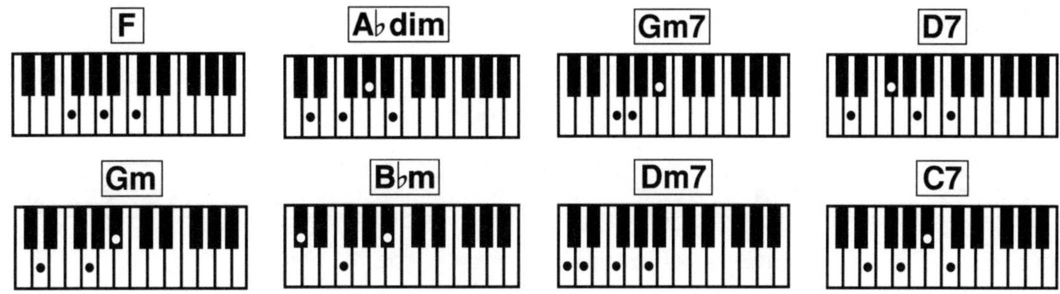
F
A♭dim
Gm7
D7
Gm
B♭m
Dm7
C7

SOMEWHERE ALONG THE WAY

Words and Music by Sammy Gallop and Kurt Adams

Suggested Registration: Flute
Rhythm: Ballad
Tempo: ♩ = 70

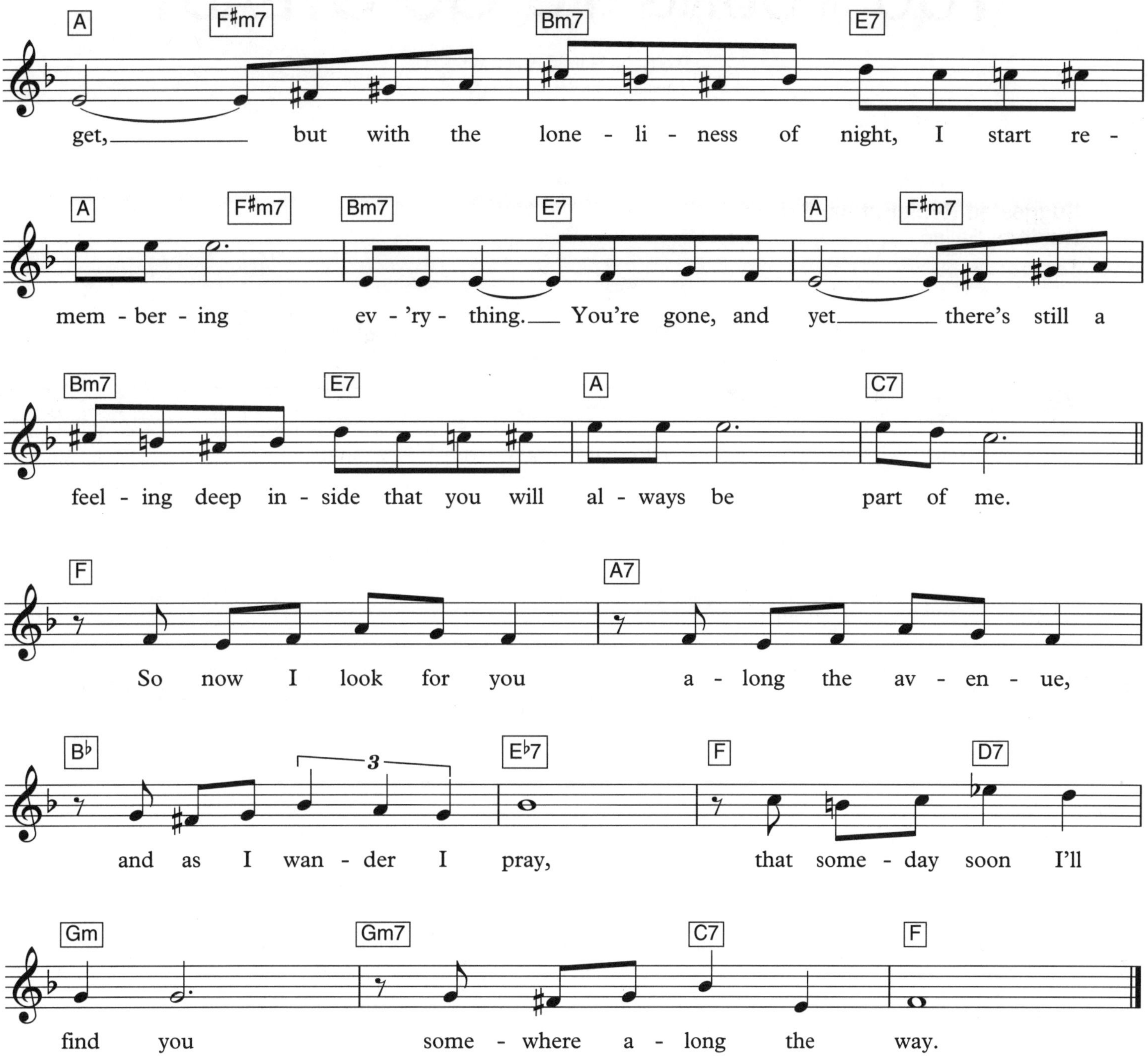

A F♯m7 Bm7 E7
get, but with the lone - li - ness of night, I start re -
A F♯m7 Bm7 E7 A F♯m7
mem - ber - ing ev - 'ry - thing. You're gone, and yet there's still a
Bm7 E7 A C7
feel - ing deep in - side that you will al - ways be part of me.
F A7
So now I look for you a - long the av - en - ue,
B♭ E♭7 F D7
3
and as I wan - der I pray, that some - day soon I'll
Gm Gm7 C7 F
find you some - where a - long the way.

F
A7
B♭
E♭7
D7
Gm
Gm7
C7
A
F♯m7
Bm7
E7

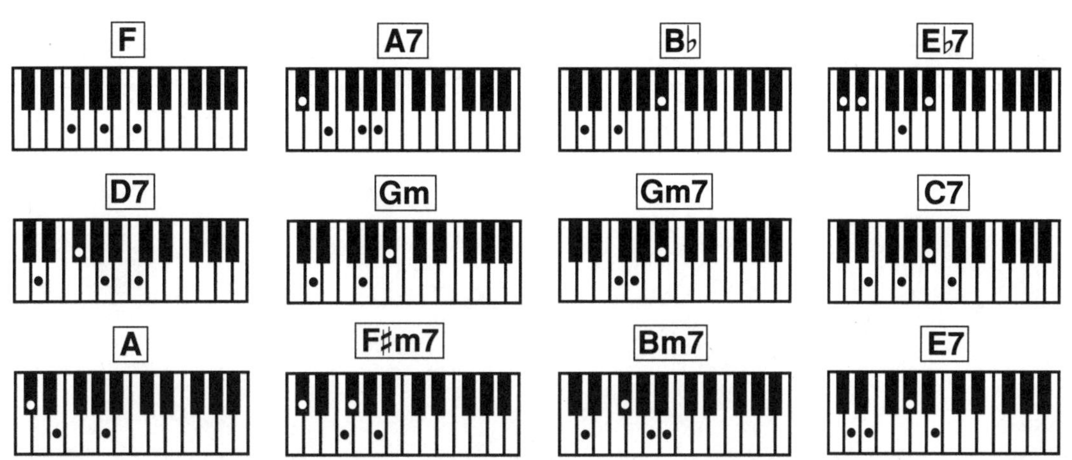

Too Young To Go Steady

Words by Harold Adamson
Music by Jimmy McHugh

Suggested Registration: Strings
Rhythm: Ballad
Tempo: ♩ = 90

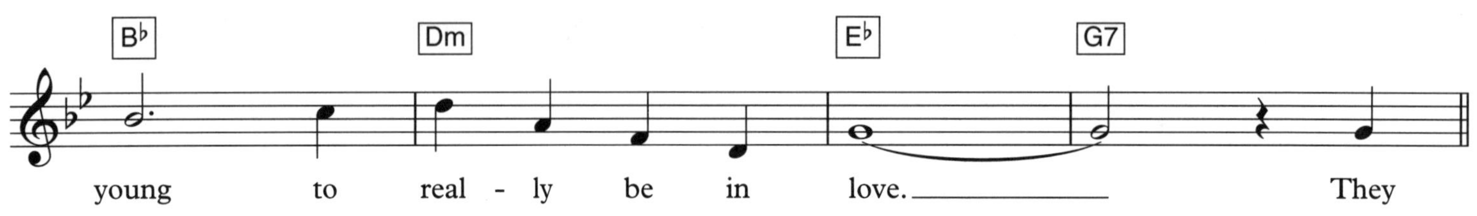

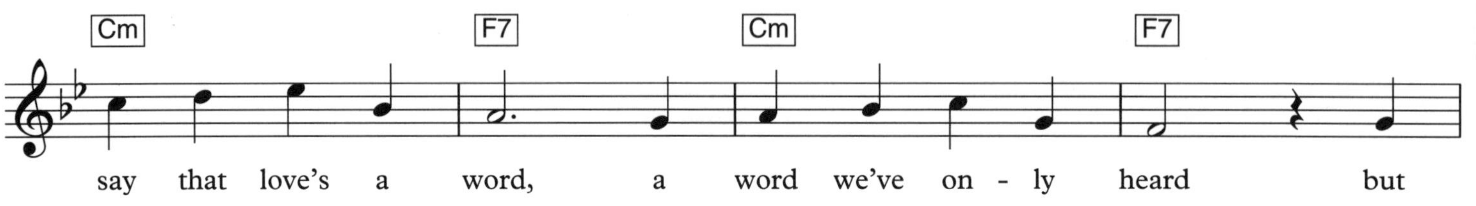

B♭
Dm
Gm
Cm7
F7
yet, we're not too young to know this

B♭
B♭7
E♭
love will last though years may go. And

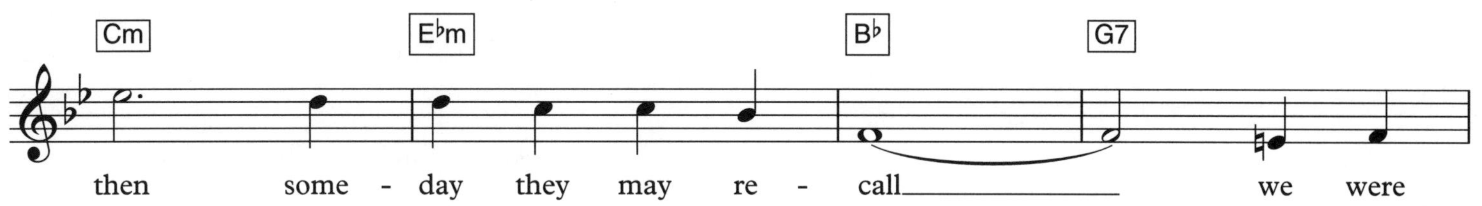
Cm
E♭m
B♭
G7
then some - day they may re - call we were

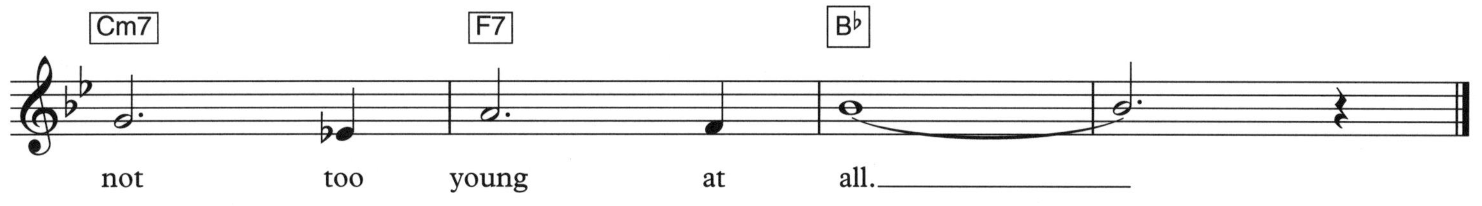
Cm7
F7
B♭
not too young at all.

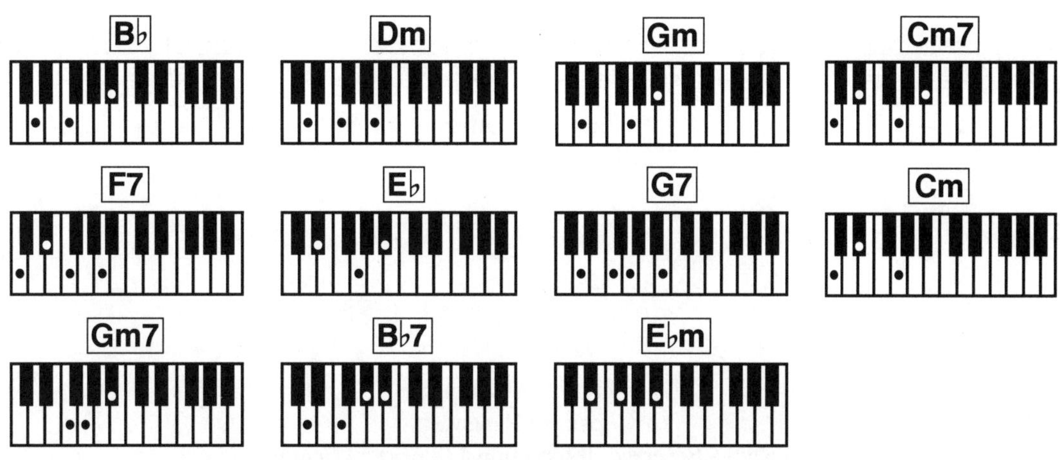
B♭
Dm
Gm
Cm7
F7
E♭
G7
Cm
Gm7
B♭7
E♭m

UNFORGETTABLE

by Irving Gordon

Suggested Registration: Strings

Rhythm: Ballad

Tempo: ♩ = 80

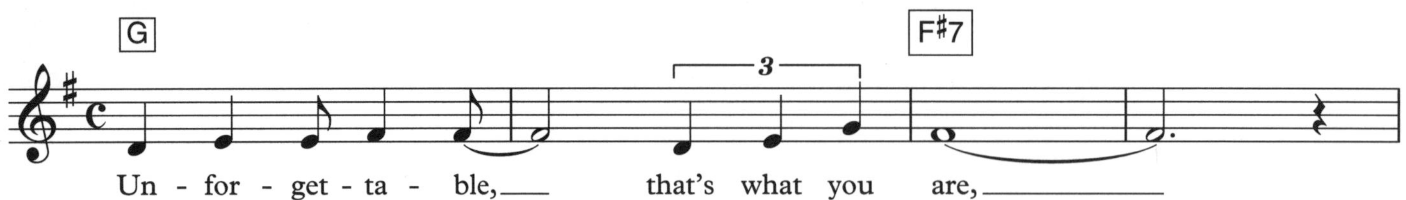

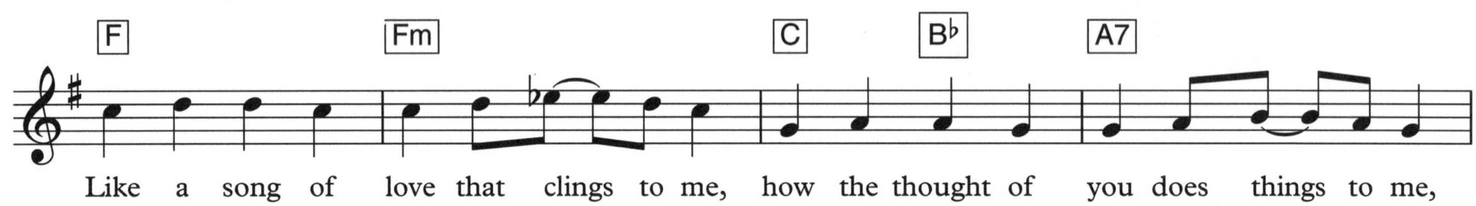

G
F♯7
3
Un - for - get - ta - ble in ev - 'ry way,

C
A7
Em7
Cm7
A7
3
and for - ev - er more, that's how you'll stay.

F
Fm
C
B♭
A7
That's why dar - ling, it's in - cred - i - ble, that some - one so un - for - get - ta - ble

Am7
D7
Dm7
G7
C
thinks that I am un - for - get - ta - ble too.

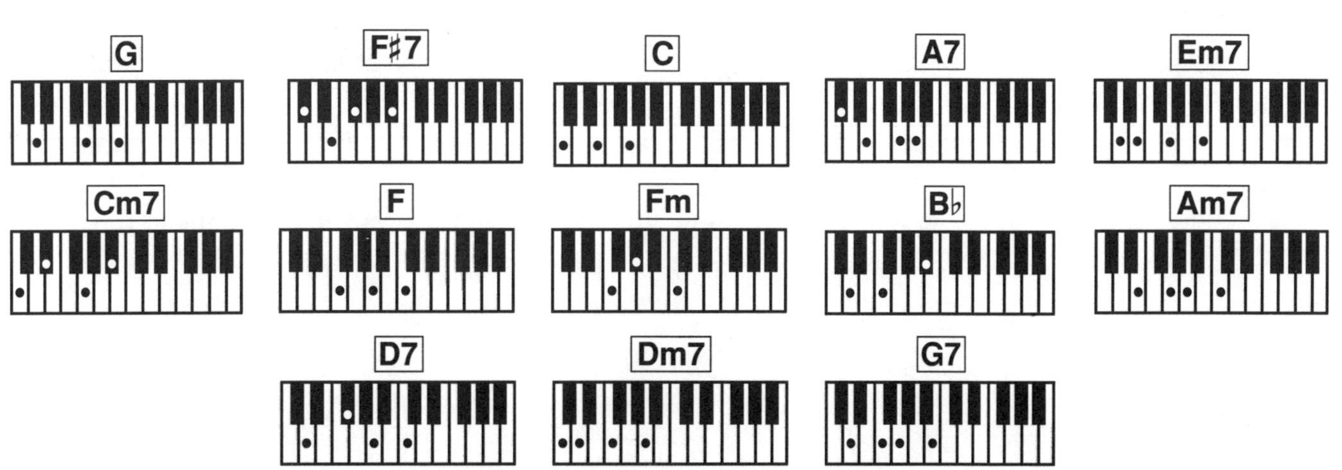

G
F♯7
C
A7
Em7
Cm7
F
Fm
B♭
Am7
D7
Dm7
G7

When I Fall In Love

Words by Edward Heyman
Music by Victor Young

Suggested Registration: Strings
Rhythm: Ballad
Tempo: ♩ = 70

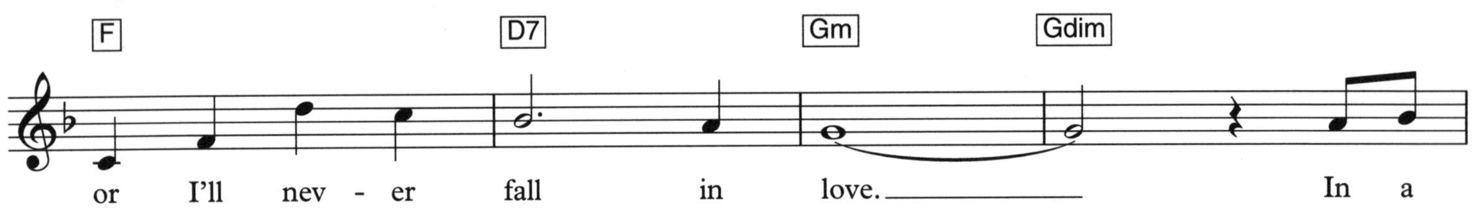

F
Gm7
C7
When I give my heart it will be com - plete - ly,

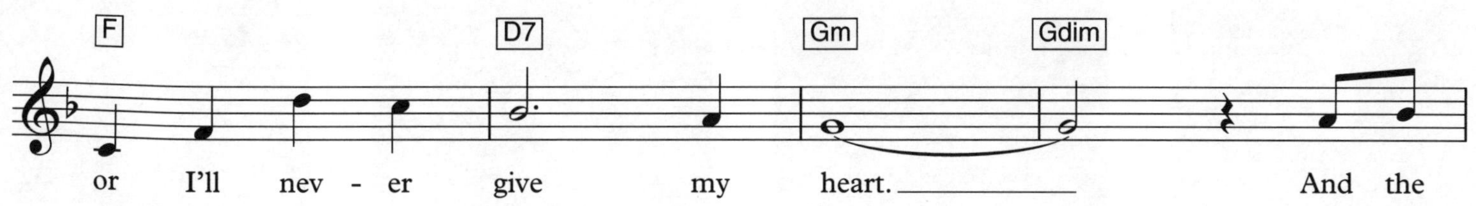
F
D7
Gm
Gdim
or I'll nev - er give my heart.
And the

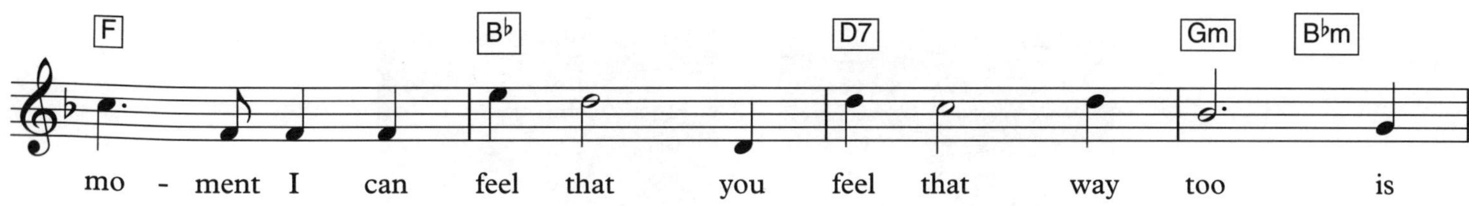
F
B♭
D7
Gm
B♭m
mo - ment I can feel that you feel that way too is

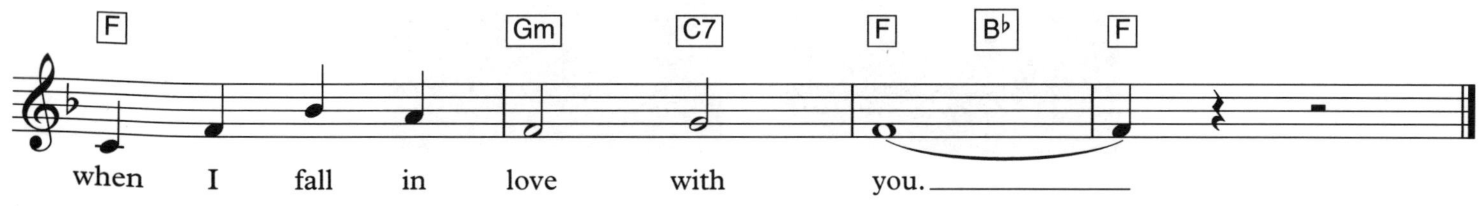
F
Gm
C7
F
B♭
F
when I fall in love with you.

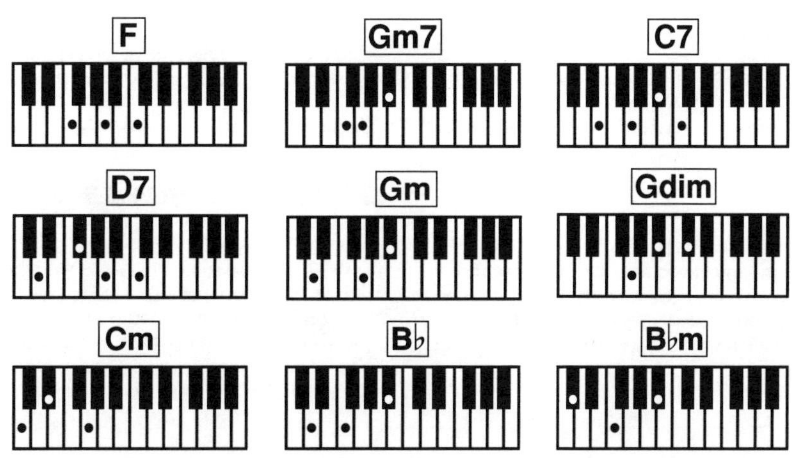
F
Gm7
C7
D7
Gm
Gdim
Cm
B♭
B♭m

LOVE SONGS

9544A E/PNO ISBN: 1-84328-115-5

Angel Of Mine - Because You Loved Me - Get Here - The Greatest Love Of All - Have I Told You Lately That I Love You - I'd Lie For You (And That's The Truth) - I Turn To You - Now And Forever - The Prayer - Right Here Waiting - The Rose - Something About The Way You Look Tonight - Unbreak My Heart - When You Tell Me That You Love Me - 2 Become 1

POP HITS

9546A E/PNO ISBN: 1-84328-117-1

Amazed - Believe - Can't Fight The Moonlight - Genie In A Bottle - Heal The World - How Do I Live - I'll Be There For You - Kiss The Rain - Livin' La Vida Loca - Macarena - Music - Quit Playing Games With My Heart - Smooth - Swear It Again - Thank You

FILM FAVOURITES

9545A E/PNO ISBN: 1-84328-116-3

Batman Theme - Beautiful Stranger - Because You Loved Me - Can You Feel The Love Tonight - Can't Fight The Moonlight - Evergreen - (Everything I Do) I Do It For You - I Don't Want To Miss A Thing - Imperial March (Darth Vader's Theme) - I Will Always Love You - Somewhere My Love (Lara's Theme) - Star Wars (Main Theme) - Superman Theme - Wind Beneath My Wings

ALL TIME GREATS

9603A E/PNO ISBN: 1-84328-138-4

American Pie – As Time Goes By – Desperado – The Greatest Love Of All – Hotel California – Lean On Me – My Heart Will Go On – My Way – Over The Rainbow – Sacrifice – Save The Best For Last – Send In The Clowns – Stairway To Heaven – Theme From New York, New York – When You Tell Me That You Love Me

GREAT SONGWRITERS

9671A E/PNO ISBN: 1-84328-175-3

As Time Goes By – Bewitched – Cabaret – High Hopes – I Got Plenty O' Nuttin' – It Ain't Necessarily So – Love & Marriage – Maybe This Time – Never Met A Man I Din't Like – Over The Rainbow – Raindrops Keep Fallin' On My Head – Send In The Clowns – Singin' In The Rain – Summertime – Tomorrow

CHRISTMAS SONGS

9790A E/PNO ISBN: 1-84328-309-3

All I Want For Christmas Is My Two Front Teeth - Deck The Hall - It's The Most Wonderful Time Of The Year - Jingle Bells - Let it Snow! Let it Snow! Let it Snow! - The Little Drummer Boy - Little Saint Nick - Have Yourself A Merry Little Christmas - I Believe In Santa Claus - The Most Wonderful Day Of The Year - O Christmas Tree - Rockin' Around The Christmas Tree - Rudolph, The Red-Nosed Reindeer - Santa Claus Is Comin' To Town - Sleigh Ride - The Twelve Days Of Christmas - Winter Wonderland

YOU'RE THE VOICE

8861A PV/CD

Casta Diva from Norma – Vissi D'arte from Tosca – Un Bel Di Vedremo from Madama Butterfly – Addio, Del Passato from La Traviata – J'ai Perdu Mon Eurydice from Orphee Et Eurydice – Les Tringles Des Sistres Tintaient from Carmen – Porgi Amor from Le Nozze Di Figaro – Ave Maria from Otello

8860A PVG/CD

Delilah – Green Green Grass Of Home – Help Yourself – I'll Never Fall In Love Again – It's Not Unusual – Mama Told Me Not To Come – Sexbomb – Thunderball – What's New Pussycat – You Can Leave Your Hat On

9297A PVG/CD

Beauty And The Beast – Because You Loved Me – Falling Into You – The First Time Ever I Saw Your Face – It's All Coming Back To Me Now – Misled – My Heart Will Go On – The Power Of Love – Think Twice – When I Fall In Love

9349A PVG/CD

Chain Of Fools – A Deeper Love Do Right Woman, Do Right Man – I Knew You Were Waiting (For Me) – I Never Loved A Man (The Way I Loved You) – I Say A Little Prayer – Respect – Think – Who's Zooming Who – (You Make Me Feel Like) A Natural Woman

9007A PVG/CD

Careless Whisper – A Different Corner – Faith – Father Figure – Freedom '90 – I'm Your Man – I Knew You Were Waiting (For Me) – Jesus To A Child – Older – Outside

9606A PVG/CD

Don't Let Me Be Misunderstood – Feeling Good – I Loves You Porgy – I Put A Spell On You – Love Me Or Leave Me – Mood Indigo – My Baby Just Cares For Me – Ne Me Quitte Pas (If You Go Away) – Nobody Knows You When You're Down And Out – Take Me To The Water

9700A PVG/CD

Beautiful – Crying In The Rain – I Feel The Earth Move – It's Too Late – (You Make Me Feel Like) A Natural Woman – So Far Away – Way Over Yonder – Where You Lead – Will You Love Me Tomorrow – You've Got A Friend

9746A PVG/CD

April In Paris – Come Rain Or Come Shine – Fly Me To The Moon (In Other Words) – I've Got You Under My Skin – The Lady Is A Tramp – My Kinda Town (Chicago Is) – My Way – Theme From *New York, New York* – Someone To Watch Over Me – Something Stupid

9770A PVG/CD

Cry Me A River – Evergreen (A Star Is Born) – Happy Days Are Here Again – I've Dreamed Of You – Memory – My Heart Belongs To Me – On A Clear Day (You Can See Forever) – Someday My Prince Will Come – Tell Him (duet with Celine Dion) – The Way We Were

9799A PVG/CD

Boogie Woogie Bugle Boy – Chapel Of Love – Friends – From A Distance – Hello In There – One For My Baby (And One More For The Road) – Only In Miami – The Rose – When A Man Loves A Woman – Wind Beneath My Wings

9810A PVG/CD

Ain't No Sunshine – Autumn Leaves – How Can I Keep From Singing – Imagine – It Doesn't Matter Anymore – Over The Rainbow – Penny To My Name – People Get Ready – Wayfaring Stranger – What A Wonderful World

9889A PVG/CD

Around The World – Born Free – From Russia With Love – Gonna Build A Mountain – The Impossible Dream – My Kind Of Girl – On A Clear Day You Can See Forever – Portrait Of My Love – Softly As I Leave You – Walk Away

10039A PVG/CD

All Of Me – Body And Soul – God Bless The Child – I Love My Man ('Billie's Blues') – Lady Sings The Blues – Lover Man (Oh Where Can You Be) – The Man I Love – My Man ('Mon Homme') – Night And Day – St. Louis Blues

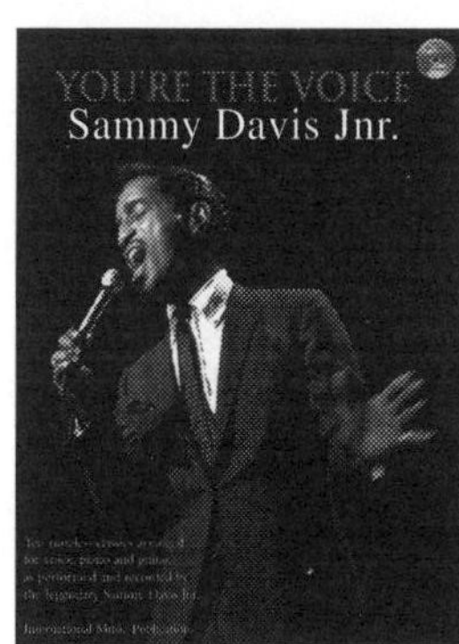

10091A PVG/CD

For Once In My Life – Hey There – It's All Right With Me – I've Gotta Be Me – Let's Face The Music And Dance – Love Me Or Leave Me – Mr Bojangles – September Song – Something's Gotta Give – What Kind Of Fool Am I?

10119A PVG/CD

Come Away With Me – Don't Know Why – Don't Miss You At All – Feelin' The Same Way – Nightingale – Painter Song – The Prettiest Thing – Sunrise – Those Sweet Words – What Am I To You?

The outstanding vocal series from IMP

CD contains full backings for each song, professionally arranged to recreate the sounds of the original recording

An expansive series of over 50 titles!

Each song features melody line, vocals, chord displays, suggested registrations and rhythm settings.

"For each title ALL the chords (both 3 finger and 4 finger) used are shown in the correct position - which makes a change!" **Organ & Keyboard Cavalcade, May 2001**

Each song appears on two facing pages eliminating the need to turn the page during performance. We have just introduced a new cover look to the series and will repackage the backlist in the same way.

Big Band Hits .19098
Blues .3477A
Broadway .9888A
Celebration Songs .3478A
Christmas Carols .4616A
Christmas Songs .19198
Classic Hits Volume 1 .19099
Classic Hits Volume 2 .19100
Cliff Richard .9030A
Cole Porter .10041A
Country Songs .19101
Disco .9394A
Eighties, The .2975A
Elton John .5779A
English Favourites .4229A
Favourite Hymns .4179A
Fifties, The .2972A
Film Classics .19197
Forties, The .2971A
Frank Sinatra .9025A
George & Ira Gershwin .9804A
George Michael .7646A
Gilbert & Sullivan .9707A
Glenn Miller .5772A
Great Songwriters .2225A
I Try Plus 10 More Chart Hits .5778A
Instrumental Classics .2338A
James Bond .9236A
Jazz Classics .5770A
Latin Collection .5777A
Love Songs Volume 1 .19102
Love Songs Volume 2 .19199
Motown Classics .2337A
Music Hall .3329A
Nineties, The .2976A
Number One Hits .19200
Number One Hits Volume 2 .9787A
Popular Classics .4180A
Pub Singalong Collection .3954A
Queen .9714A
Robbie Williams Easy Keyboard .9501A
Rock 'n' Roll Classics .2224A
Scott Joplin .9738A
Seventies, The .2974A
Shirley Bassey .9350A
Showtunes Volume 1 .19103
Showtunes Volume 2 .3328A
Sixties, The .2973A
Soft Rock Collection .4617A
Soul Classics .19201
Thirties, The .2970A
Traditional English Favourites .4229A
Traditional Irish Favourites .4230A
Traditional Scottish Favourites .4231A
TV Themes .19196
Twenties, The .2969A
Wartime Collection .3955A
Wedding Collection .3688A
Whitney Houston .7647A